Appetite for the Divine

Christine Gelineau

The Ashland Poetry Press
Ashland University
Ashland, Ohio 44805

Printed in the United States of America

ISBN: 978-0-912592-68-8

Library of Congress Catalog Card Number: 2009911870

Cover design by Janine Gelineau

Photograph by Ryan S. Gregor

Cover image is a detail of *Eve Tempted*, modeled 1839–1842, carved 1873–1877, by Hiram Powers; marble 68 7/8 x 29 7/8 x 20 1/2 in. (174.9 x 75.8 x 52.0 cm.) Smithsonian American Art Museum

For my family,

and in memory of my father,
Gilbert E. Gelineau
(1919–1997)

Contents

Between the hammer strokes our hearts survive
like the tongue that between the teeth
and in spite of everything
goes on praising.

Rilke, *The Ninth Duino Elegy*

Counter-Love

.

.

.

.

.

.

■

Before

we knew we were blind we
had motion

■

■

wand of
the arm in the amnion ~
fish thrash

thrumming the delicious
ripple of ribs: the firmament
beyond that inapparent sky

■

■

The fetus in that
world of sound and motion
seemingly complete
■
practices appetite
■

■

expelled   newborn   the suck
begins at once   that
hunger we have
for one another
■
communicant of
the mother's blood
and body arrives
here in air wholly
famished
■

3

.
.
.

The head crowns
forcing the petalled labia out
     into a wide-mouthed
       astonished O

      a thin-lipped corona
    about the emerging black star

                .
                .
                .

            light blooms
       on retinas which until now have known
           .
    only darkness   and thus have failed
           .
      to sense that in which they
were so fully immersed.

           .

.
.
.
.

What do we know so completely now
    .
   as we knew darkness then
    .
   that its presence is
    .
   our wholest absence?
    .
    .

.
.
.
.

Black bear on the April island
snuffles for corn
.
.
inhabiting
this moment of wintered-
over field corn between the paws
.
so fully it has the feel
.
of everlasting
.
.
.
Spring now is a thin tune

beginning

in the branches

.
.
.

.
.
.

Slow softening
southern air eases
the crystal season.
.

in fields, each flake
anticipates the yield,
the song long held

pressed out now in underlayer
lyric as the snow
compresses upon itself;

roof edges leak
to the opening banks beneath,
a fluidity

unsensed in
stiff furious storm
and still of winter.

.
.

Over fields
a white wheel of
wings returns

.
.

the clustered horses
raise buoyant heads
to the scent.

.

■
■
■

Torn from deep space
into the chaos of contrasts
■

the planetary infant arches
into the ragged shape of the limbed
■
■

new moon of stunned flesh   the infant
rests against the gravid mother
■

■
captured and supported while
the tie to the past is severed
■
and hands towel away the clouded
swirls of vernix from the blue
translucence of the skin
now a transformed fragment
■
healed into the circle of the mother's arms
new voice stilled against her breast
■

the infant hoods his eyes and
sucks in awareness with the milk:
■
warmth
wetness
■
satiation
■

impermanence
■

.
.
.

unconditional as earth
.
.
.

the mother is complete
.
.
.

in the incompleteness of perception
.
.
.

.
.
.

.
.
.

.
.
.

earth in April is unfinished
as an infant skull:
.
a fontanel
uncovered by membrane opens in the field
.
.
.

the liquid song
of underlayer rushing pulls you:
.
.
.

drawn like the saint to the resurrected
you dip a finger in to feel
the steady music of that pulse
.
.
.

rills of silver running through the rocks
.
the flow of
counter-love   original response:
.
how we come to love the world

.
.
.

The Dream of Rivers

.

.

.

.

.

■

Throughout
　　the dream of rivers hums
　　　　the assurance of ocean:

　　　　the magnetism
of destination
　　is the dream of rivers

　　　　it roars Niagara

　　　　　　that alluring
　　　　　　silver free-fall
　　　　　　purer
　　　　　　than intent

　　　　　the lyric release that lasts
　　　　　the moment's ever-after

that pellucid falling
　　　　goes on endlessly

　its sharded end against stone
　　　　　　likewise

　　　　　　　　endless

■

■

■

.

.

.

The maple in October
is emotional with leaves
gushing out in gold

as if desire could be enough.
.

.

Nightly now
we eat the dying garden
down, harvest a sharp

tang on the tongue.

.

.

.

■

■

■

Euarctos americanus   the American black bear
plantigrade as a   human
the whole of the sole and all five toes flat
to the ground so that the imprint
is familiar   touchingly
pudgy   the wedge of sole and
petalling of toes we have learned
to associate with safety   ease
infants and sunny beaches

the appeal here is deceptive
each toe hollow punctuated
with the pock from a claw:
a paw whose single blow
can kill you

I pull my boot   my shoe   my sock   to sign
my foot there beside the bear track
in the icy suck of snow

slender   arched   the delicate moon
prints of toes express a neat
unpunctuated   row

the April snow so unequivocally
cold

■

■

■

15

.
.

Time too
has its seamless disjunctions:

                the photographs in my father's G.I.
        photo album are grainy gray   my own
                progenitor in his twenty-fifth spring
            among his buddies   among the bombed-out ruins
        his rifle slung from his shoulder with the same
    easy familiarity I'd seen baby sister's diaper bag ride there.

The photos were chiefly taken
at war's end   the sucked-down
soldiers' smiles more
relieved than triumphant

                there's Dad at Lucerne   Dad at Wiesbaden
            then folded in behind the last stack
                    as if tucked
                    up against memory's inner eyelid

        were the photos he shot
        the May morning they
        liberated Mauthausen

                    A camera is both
                    record and bulwark
                    It stills
                    and contains light

        the eye   the hand   which photographed me
        in my mother's arms   my bassinet   my bath
        That eye   that hand   connect me still to the sunlight
        disinterestedly soaking the orderly stacks of corpses as
        my father photographs Mauthausen

                    the long-ago light staining
            the film   with incurious accuracy

                                                .
                                                .

．

．

．

May morning after rain:
the meadow
unreasonably green
and strewn about with
the coronas
of dandelions

unexpectedly

the flock of flowers lifts

into the wavering
flight of finches

then the yellow
finches weave
over the astral meadow

a mesh
of motion
in the gold-soaked air.

．

．

．

.

.

.

      The rubbery hieroglyphics
   of skid marks on the highway
      tell the suddenness

            of arriving where
                  we never believed
         we were headed

.

.

.

.

.

.

the air at Niagara
        is vibrant with oxygen the mist
        releases

                newlyweds
        and suicides intoxicate
on the cataract's

        awful sublimity:

the tale the water tells
    against the stones is steadier
            than the stones themselves

.

.

.

Natural History

·

·

·

·

·

    ■

    ■

buoyant
    in the bob
and roil of the sea

    ■

    ■

    the
cormorant
    rocks   serene

    ■

    ■

the ocean is earth
    in fast-forward

all the motion   manifest
    ■

    ■

wholly apparent here
    how ascent
    ■
and descent
rise / fall from one another
    ■
are one another
    ■

.
.

Maut Hausen   :   Toll House

the Austrian citizens there practiced incuriosity

.
.
.

Until 1939 the Castle Hartheim housed the handicapped
under the care of the Merciful Sisters

.

The Nazis temporarily
displaced   the defective
children   the nuns
while the castle was refitted

.

plumbed for gas
by discreet Austrians with families to feed
and control of their emotions

.
.
.

Bussed back
the retarded children waved
when they thought they glimpsed
the altar boy who'd served at the castle's daily Mass
youngsters headed home   happy

.

by evening smoke
            and the occasional
                     tuft
                        of hair
      — a child's tendrils lifting
                           in a breeze—
breached the chimney and

.

escaped alone to the village streets

24

■

■

■

It is not darkness then
    which incites the infant's cry
        but hollowness.
                ■
The mother's body   her
warmth   her pulse
            can reshape the night
                ■
hold off
        the palpable hungering of
            everything which waits

                suspending

        the two

                ■

who recover
    if only for the moment
                ■
    in the eucharist of the breast
        and   mouth together
                ■
        this grateful sharing
    in the rocking dark

                ■

                ■

                ■

．

the apple tree
　　　　is virginal again

baptized
　　　in blossoms

　　　　　　　not
　　　petalled over in
boughten goods but

　　　　　uncovered　　drawn out
　　　　　　　somewhere from the heart

　　　　　　a skin
　　　a bridal dress of purity

brought forth
　　　　clean as light and loud
　　with the lusty solicitudes
　　　　　　of bees

．

．

．

26

.

.

unexpected
      and perishable as insight

I wake to find the lenses

    of my myopic eyes have
        inexplicably recalled

perfect

curvature:
    every specific shape

    in the room
        crisp

    newly-

defined.

.

.

    Wide-eyed I strain

to maintain the vision
      knowing

the inevitability of eyelids
    .
    that gentle sweep
    .

that wipes the old
      flawed world

    back into view.
    .

．
．
．
．

the warm
and animate dark

．
．

hums its accustomed
lullabye

．
．

of nourishing

and devouring

．
．

■

■

Wide-voiced valley in darkness:
amniotic   dream-swollen the
eager river sings
across
her boundaries
open
tuneful in the
windrows

■

she swells the pastures
licks
the fence posts out
and sets the wire humming

■

the river washes into yards
across the patterning
of those who see themselves
resisting

■

she laps the porch
and carries furniture away

■

■

wide wild menstrual music
a cleansing flow internally
demanded

■

beneath
cold tapestry of stars
the silver river's making song
of so much
alteration

■

■

Time Is the Flame

■

■

■

■

■

.

.

.

In the measure of an ant's life
what moment could compare to this?

        suspended in a bellows of blue light
        treading a causeway of living petal

            tracing the inner labia of a sunlit
            iris with the tender whisper

       of its cilia-fine legs

    aloft
       in an atmosphere of bloom

           .

           .

           .

.

.

.

Moon swims the night haze, pale
carp in an umber sea. The man

watching thinks *soft
as a ripe pear, lush*

as a peony. Cancer has
bitten him down to a bone hook.

Blade of a man now he waits
in the languid, chirruping dark,

a honed lure drifting
in reach of the moon's

unappeasable hunger.

.

.

.

.

.

        astute students of their century
    the Argentine death squads of the 1970s
        were successful for a decade
    in a deft shell game of submerged terror:

your daughter is not here:
perhaps the rebel forces . . .
are you sure your son was not a subversive?
Your daughter even now we believe is in hiding

while yards away, as officials knew full well,
 her son the musician
swung his chains into melodies
        shaping time's blank stare
      into what meaning he could come to
       .

       .

    Time
  to the mother whose child has been lost
    is a heavy surplus   as if
the child's long unused span
    were suddenly her own to make sense of.
       .

       .

In the burden of time
the mothers of the erased generation
        work the names of their lost along the borders
    of their *panuelos*, the embroidered letters
    vivid against the chill white of the shawls.

.
.
.
.

                    Is this Thursday?
            under the Buenos Aires sun
            in the Plaza de Mayo mothers
            are circling the obelisk linked
            hand to hand in a single embrace
                    Argentina's *madwomen*
                    implacable as snow

.
.

．
．

a black man
    a tall, handsome
a tall handsome black man is
    a black man is singled out
    ．

singled out by other blacks,
    singled out by strangers

a tall, handsome black man is singled out
by strangers who
    ．

    for reasons which need not
be named   for reasons which
cannot be named,
    reasons which cannot
be defended
    other blacks, strangers
    select him
    ．

"He resisted but he did not fight."
    ．

That caption went
with the photo of two men
    sticking small knives into
the one man's skull.
    ．

The text fills in
    they pierced his chest and belly as well,
while the tall man crawled,
    crawled from them
    the strangers whose
reasons cannot be defended
    ．

.

poured the petrol,
anointed him, and lit the match.
.

He leapt up
illuminated.
.

.

.

In the final
photo we
see him there   ascending from the earth,
.

burdened with the flame upon his back,

but rising

.

.

.

■

■

oaks open their solicitous burgundy palms
in the slant light of early November
diffidently beseechful
■

■

in the bronzed cauldron of the valley, locust
trees test the wind with the bloodied
tongues of their leaves
■

■

crimson-stippled maples float in that Pentecostal
murmuring   press themselves to one
another, press intimately to the earth

■

■

■

.
.

A wood stove reminds you
what it is you have
brought into the home
each time you unlatch
the door and thrust the dead
weight bundle of a log
into the roil
of that indifferent heart.

Backing out of the drive
on some errand or another you
look back to the house and hope
to read reassurance in the blue
whistle of smoke the chimney exhales,
but carry the gnaw of worry
with you nonetheless:

in your mind the house
could already be engulfed,
the fire poised in that critical instant
of barbaric elegance
when the flame shapes to the fuel
it is consuming, the house transfigured
to a structure of livid light,
the very image of your losses.

That imagined radiance compels

the mind far beyond any

refutations you can invent

fueled by the certainty that

time is the flame

and no one ever
returns to the home they left.

.

.

.

■

■

The crocus then
■

■

is more reliable than hope

■

■

■

Ordinary Time

- .
- .
- .
- .
- .

．

．

Night wind licks your upturned face and its chill
tastes intimate
and unreachable as if
it had blown in from the aloof constellations
．

．

you are buoyed
held
in the impartial amnion of that black
air
．

．

your face cupped now in the palms
of the night's appreciation of night
．

cherished as wholly as any lover
whose face is held to the other's like a mirror
a hollowed   hallowed   source

．

．

．

.

.

the heretofore-unvisited
blackberry bramble
is networked with corridors
which open
into the thicket's
fruiting centers
.

fitted now into the curious
cleared socket which pushes
back the brambles exactly
the distance my arm needs
to reach among the thorns and grasp
the soft pulse of berries:
.

I gather
the juicy black suns
and consider
the already-emptied cones
of fruit I had not picked which
nonetheless
are gone
.

while my heart beats steadily
its ancient suggestion:
bears eat berries
bears eat berries
.

the hairs at the back
of my neck ruffle
in the lilt
of that hymn

.

.

■

■

■

What satiation would Eve have imagined
as her teeth cleaved the apple?

■

Was the choice really between death
and an eternity of self-limitation?

■

Is death a punishment
or a gift we misunderstand?

■

What were we made for
if not this appetite for the divine?

■

■

■

．

．

The Jews of Mauthausen stepped
        into the air
            over the quarry

        singly at first
    then linked
        hand to hand   the first man
                leapt
    and the ribbon of Jews
        jerked with him over the lip
                ．
            flown free
            two hundred
            sixty feet
        to the frank
        granite below
                ．
            Jew after Jew
        in a cascade
    of flight

            ．

        the clean
    and pitiless air
        of Austria

                    vibrates
                        still

            ．

            ．

48

■

■

Nothing could have been
more accidental
or more formative
than my father's wartime years

Taught to fly and speak Finnish
he was sent to France and Austria with the infantry

In Finnish he can still count to ten
and ask for cigarettes   a cocktail party trick

but flying fixed forever his underlying sense
of the world's true face:

that immaculate
mathematic grace of landscape

so tangible from the cockpit canopy
the curve of the horizon
comforting as
the cheek of the beloved

an orderliness as irrefutable as instinct

an image so magnetic
even the war failed to dissemble it

■

■

·

·

The handsome adventurer works in movies
a celluloid Superman
but he recreates with horses   high-strung elastic jumpers
unpredictable as the fortunes of movie stardom
·

snapped suddenly to the ground
one day when the horse   balks   his life   the watching wife's life
unspooling   remaking themselves in the whipcrack
of that spin through air
·

the multiply-fractured vertebrae in the neck
ravage the spinal cord   end
corporeality   while mortality
is held artificially off by the respirator
·

What could it mean to live
isolated in the unhoused brain
with even
the animal lub-dub of your own heart
sublime
and remote as a planet?
·

unburdened as the angels
·

held back only by your own desire
your own stubborn hungering
to remain connected still
to that which dies

·

·

·

■

■

The butterflies are drying
  their newly opened wings in the sun
        clinging
    in the breeze to crumbs
  of soil and grass blades
  ■

If cognition were possible
  wouldn't terror be the first response
  to the pageantry of wings grown
from your own back   tugging
   lifting you into the wind
  ■

   anxious as any being
borne out
   of its known world?

■

■

The Appearance of Meaning

.

.

.

.

.

In this August meadow,
     windrows of new-mown
     hay cure under
the summer sun:

the farmer waits,

     his arms pinned
          in the maw of the metaphor,
          his arms

extended into the baler
     he'd been trying to unjam,

jammed now with him,
     the whole of his young man arms
          lost, the mangle
     of the rollers tight
as a tourniquet
     so that he
          is not lost, he

survives

     to carry for years
the afternoon's wisdom

in the memory of his arms.

■

■

What would *God* mean
        if not *apprehender?*
                ■

                        ■

The irresistible
        sense of witness
that is Psyche's oxygen:
                ■

God's steadfastness as Reader
calls us into language
                ■

that vivifying legerdemain
which cannot withhold infusing
its signs with uncanny activity:
                ■

the shine
of that suggestive action shimmering
                to be read
                ■

                ■

        what else would any god
long for from us?

                ■

                ■

                ■

                ■

Our daughters have become orchards,
petalled and fragrant as light.
.
In the agile branches brash song
and incandescent orioles.
.
It is their turn to be divine now
while we grow more mortal
.
every day. We wake to the ash
of dreams upon our tongues, and catch
.
the intermittent scent of accidents
and inevitable calamities we have yet
.
to suffer, yes, our throats swell
with the vibrato of everything we've
.
been compelled to know, but today
beneath the red-nippled trees, long-haired
.
meadow grasses shiver and daffodils
gesture the lithe hands of their fronds.
.
Let the heart twist like a flower breaking
into blossom, lasting is not all.

.

.

.

Physicists infer we perceive
perhaps a single percent
of what they believe
to be there
.

"dark matter" they call
the un-sensable 99 percent

.

How small the light
how deep the hunger

.

.

.

■
■

In darkness it begins :

                He stands in the surge
          and retreat of the sea :
                the unremitting inspire /
          expire of the surf's
                swallowing :   casts out
          the glint, the live bait
                of his own hunger to hook
          that silver muscle of what we know
                to lurk there, nearly out of reach :

          slowly dawn smudges the horizon

     ■
     ■

stripped : striped : strike:

               the line keens out of the reel
               like a shriek, the jerk and rush
               of that filament all he sees
               of the struggle : knowledge now
               a province of the body not the
               intellect : he holds clear
               of the frantic line and grips
               the shuddering rod two-handed
               as it pulls him deeper : he plays
               the live line :   deeper
               but diagonal, holding

as best he can to the shallows,
the shore, the electricity
of that filament steady now :
thrusting with an energy pure
as any desire

.
.

stripped : struck : strung

Desire is tireless but the flesh
is not :   the glitter of menhaden
with a hook for a heart :   the bite
and drag of it :   the exhausting
tease of the man's grip and release :
closer to shore :   closer
to shore :   hauled towards
the light :   the fire
of oxygen   :   air

: beached :

whose element the amnion :
whose exertion the victory?
fish the length of the man's
toddler daughter : the mylar
glitter of the scales : the eye :
fading even as the glistering
water drips from the body
back into the sea

.

.

.
.
.

The solidity dailiness
appears to possess
 is a quality we amass

         .
scrubbing the toilet   sorting
trousers from underwear   lifting
our child down from the swing   idling
at the intersection   reading recipes
filing reports pushing carts
down grocery aisles making
    love to our spouse,

            washing those sheets

        then drying them in the sun
                        .

                        .

            Given
    time enough we at last realize how
          it must come to this
        gradual putting off of gravity
                    .

        how even the skull, the bones
        hollow out of their density

              release
                    like light   rising

                        .

                        .

                        .

．

On the feral hillside
the honeybee hunts the
blush pink cups of applebloom
on the undomesticated bough.

．

The electric zum of its membranous wings
weaves a strand of sound into
the hoarse-throated hum
of highway noise, that persistent
human undertone palpable
these three miles distant.

．

As limited as that :
one bee in the blooms
of an untamed apple :

．

in the soft May twilight
the satisfaction
is profound:

．

this appearance
of meaning
beyond our meanings.

．

．

What Holiness Is Left Us

.

.

.

.

.

■

■

My children named no one
during torture. The proof of this
is that many
of their friends are still alive. My children
did not speak.

To resist
perhaps they thought of love
but I do not
want to imagine
what my children thought of during torture.

They believed the world would change.

What they did not know was
that it would be the rush
of their own blood
that would change it.

I don't want to be the mother of Christ.

■

■

■

■

■

When we reach the border they
will ask us, what
■
have you to declare
■
the night sky's lone eye
    rolls back
■
remorseless
as the dream of elsewhere

■

■

■

■

■

Even as I dreamed it the dream felt like a movie:
the slope of the paddock
down to the two outbuildings was not
the lay of our land, the three-rail board
fence not the cheap electric that encircles
our pastures, the sheds unlike any
buildings we have ever had.
■

But in the dream we owned the landscape
and our gelding Chad was sunfishing in the air
as he has been known to do and then galloping to the far corner
by the sheds to confront the intruder.
The horse he challenged in the corner
of the paddock was not a horse I recognized
dark   tall   bulky as a draft horse
and cocked to kick.   That's when
■

■

the shed burst into flame,
                first a glow in the open doorway
but rapidly engulfed and suddenly stepping
out of the doorway a figure :   the shape of a flaming man
detaches from the other flame
waving his arms as if to brush off
the fire that enveloped him.   *Where is Stephen?*
I think, at the same instant

67

that it seems to me I know the flame-man
now implausibly wading back *into* the fire
is not Stephen but the vagrant sometimes hired for odd chores.

.

In our waking lives, there is no vagrant,
but here in the movie-dream he is
livid and lost. Stephen runs from the barn I hadn't before
noticed, up the hill behind me.   He has seen
no figure, only the roaring shed
and I say, "All the horses are out."

.

I don't say, "There's a man inside."

.

I am convinced the man is long past
hope and I don't want Stephen taking
any risks on his behalf and so,
I say only "Call 911"

.

After the clang and clamor,
when the shed is a blackened space of smolder and smoke
and the remains have been discovered, I consider
what I could say, what I could acknowledge

.

but I say   nothing
the burning man walking from the fire,
his worried gesturing,
his walking back in. Over and over in the silence.

.

.

■

■

Chaos is the material of creation
     the fabric of fabrication
     the stew
     ■
       of generation
     ■
generous
     and vital   chaos seeks
         ■
        coming apart
and coming together   equally urgently
        ■

        make
      and re-make
        ■
the systole-diastole of the cosmos
the embrace endlessly separate

     and whole

■

■

■

■

■

.

our surprise is
deeply felt   and unsupportable
when we recognize the barbarians at the gate

as our own children bone of our bone
cocking the stolen rifles   lining the victims up
in the tender crosshairs of the scope

■

■

in the country's heartland
the soil is black   and deep
the trees
are entering the earth
as coffins

■

■

■

■

.

.

Adolph   :   Hermann   :   Eva
Mothers who suckled Nazis at their breast
        named with the same
        anticipation as anyone

.

.

Itzak   :   Helena   :   Abram :   Ruth   :
        Annelise   :   Laure   :   Eli   :   Samuel   :
Benjamin   :   Leah   :   Moshe   :
Edith   :   Nikolaus   :   Rolf   :   Esther   : Jelena   :

.

.

        the meticulously
            recorded coil:

.

.

    unraveling in the atmosphere

    mixing with the ash
of Hiroshima   Nagasaki   raining

.

        on us still

.

    In the newsreel films we watch
    fifty years after the camps' liberation
        it is the liberators' faces
        which are joyous

    the apparent promise
    of rescuing from the rubble:
                conflating salvage
            with salvation

.

.   71

.

.

.

Pressed by the weight
of our hope   the gate exhales

into green-black landscape:
a heard thought

The sandy road
beneath us is texture, not interpretation:

pooled in moonlight, patient
and urgent as poetry

the road that waits before us
is fisted in prayer

.

.

.

Common Prayer

.

.

.

On ultrasound the two-fifths-formed
fetus spins   balletic
                        supple
                            .
        suffused with a deftness
our clumsy land bodies
                    somehow never
                        can wholly relinquish
            the memory of
                        .
                individual
                        cells dissolve
    slough off   absorb
                        .
            we are nowhere
        who we were
                        .
                    and yet
        that buoyancy we knew first
                    lingers
                        .
                imprinted
        deeper than thought
                        .

            persistent   as desire

                        .

                        .

Here in air   abandon
                and precision are
the two faces of a single minting:
                exactitude,
            as any skater,
                any poet knows,
                    .
        is a kind of fervor:
                    .

            passion, that uncharted dive into self
        that leads out of the flooded cave
                into the ocean beyond self, yes
                    .

                    but thought, too, can lead to unthought:
skilled practice melting at last to some
            sweet recovered moment
        of the fetus's lost acceptance of one's own flesh
                    .
                    .

    we float there secure
            in the encompassing support   the caress
                    of flesh's own element :
                        mortality

                    .

                    .

                    .

                    .

∎

∎

The magazine relates an incident a reader has witnessed:
crowded intersection in Texas at rush hour;
two Hueys flying into the area for an air show:
enormous   apian thwap
overhead   unmistakably darkening
pulsating
the Texas afternoon
∎

a business-suited man leaves
his BMW in the lane,
a biker parks his Harley on the shoulder
and the two stand together in the suddenly
paused intersection
hands raised in salute
in the shiver of memory
∎

until the Hueys whap resolutely past
shrinking into the blue

∎

∎

∎

∎

■

■

In his stall the movie star's horse
    wickers for his evening grain
      ■

        eager
   in his acceptance
      of things as they are.

■

■

.

.

Do we ever
experience death as anything
except an impact?
.

dropping through a darkness whose polestar
was the flames consuming what had been
their plane
did they think they had already died?
.

did they claw at that black air
or dive
for the irresistible merging?
.

Picture them lying back in sudden acceptance
—almost a serenity—
propelled like Benjamin's angel into history's stream
eyes fixed on the blare of the past's calamity,
wings pinioned in the onrush
of the future's inconsolable embrace
.

.

.

.

■

■

In this
    the refugee's century
our ears are stoppered
with the death wails of the forgotten

■

■

The sound that filters
through the howling of the dispossessed
    is a deep-throated silence
like the straited roar
    in a seashell's inner whorls

■

■

■

■

■

■

Why did they attack now?
    the commentator asks
    the field correspondent

        They felt they could.
        Their forces are superior.

■

■

．

．

．

In my line of sight on awakening
the window defines two oblongs

of undifferentiated light —a diffuse
whiteness which suggests neither

rebuke
nor invitation

I choose to believe
there is still space
and time

．

．

State of Grace

.

.

.

.

.

·

·

the angels move among
the living and the dead
Rilke said   making little distinction
the veil between the realms
membranous
osmotic
sucking through to death
tenderly   hungry
as a kiss
·

·

What kind of love blossoms like this
with sudden vividness
into bombs?

cars a twist   smoldering   high
rise buildings sheared
like an embrace which can never
be repeated   a thumb
scalp scraps   re-rod   computers
legs   up-ended furniture   the baby

peels
                                    in crimson
          apart

petals

          in the would-be rescuer's arms

·

·

.

.

Hawk on extended
wing
describes
the inapparent
air
.

The mind's
most dangerous trick is
to imagine itself detached
.
from the body which
expresses it

free
of the web:

.

the raptor's mortal
grace is an
interwoven communion:
seed to shrew to hawk to fertile decomposition
and back
to new seed
the everlastingly mutable
present

.

.

.

.

Each of us is susceptible to the misimpression
that we are walking about
in the world

.

when
what we walk about in
is the version
of the world we're prepared
to perceive

.

This is not excuse
or explanation
but limitation

.

jaws against which
one should struggle with

.

the instinctive fury
of any trapped thing

.

.

■

■

Waking the morning after watching
Schindler's List to the sound
of the TV downstairs tuned
to CNN: American-born
Jewish settler in Hebron slaughters
Muslims at their prayers
in his zeal to pervert
the peace process

blood promising promising promising
as it soaks into clothing   runs onto
stones while my daughter's
radio plays Mary Chapin Carpenter singing
Passionate Kisses :   *shouldn't I have this*
        shouldn't I have this, shouldn't I
    have all of this, and . . .
■
The slaughterer is a trained
medical doctor   his omniscience
localized as any particular dying
■
The radio plays in an empty room
 news telling itself old
telling itself to itself   complete
    in the incompleteness of
    its unreceived telling

passionate kisses
evaporate unremarked
in the omnivorous air

■

■

.

.

.

in the trimming that makes the answer true
        truth   is lost
                .

.

    In the absence
            of answers   meaning
        may yet find space
                to emerge

.

.

.

.

■

■

shouldn't the antiquity of our suffering
amount to more?

■

■

I remain
    distracted by hope

■

■

■

■

＊

＊.

the pulmonary worms
open airways in
the breathing body of the earth

a delicate lace
of absence in
the seemingly solid presence of dirt

＊

ants trace the surface   carrying
specks of formicidian manna from
one realm to the other while amongst

their efforts the newborn colt
pulls tender slips of the green grass April draws
from his granddam's grave

＊

all the earth is animate
with the dreams
of the unnumberable buried

the scattered   the decayed:
humus is rich with memories
diatomaceous recollections

＊

That earth which supports
and calls to us
with such hungry affection

echoes now as the mare and foal
in the sunshine   in their state of grace canter
their hooves raising

an interconnecting
cardiac cadence from
within the echoing ground.

.
.

Notes

The epigraph is from David Young's translation of Rainer Maria Rilke's *Duino Elegies*. The line breaks which worked for Young in the elegies as a whole did not work with this excerpt so I have translated his line to my own page, much as Young did to /for Rilke.

p. 9 *counter love   original response* The phrase is Robert Frost's, from his poem "The Most of It." I encountered the line first in a volume of Eleanor Wilner's poems, and only much later looked up the Frost poem.

p. 35 This section is based on the words of Father Luis Angel Farinello, a priest in Buenos Aires and one time third-world activist known for his work in social justice. Father Farinello's words were recorded by Eric Stener Carlson in Carlson's book *I Remember Julia: Voices of the Disappeared.* Temple University Press, Philadelphia, 1996.

p. 65 These are the words of Renee Epelbaum, an Argentinean mother whose three children, Luis, Claudio and Lila, were all kidnapped and never seen again. The prisoner who made music with his chains (p. 35) was believed to have been Claudio Epelbaum. Information on the Epelbaums was taken from *The Mothers of Plaza De Mayo: The Story of Renee Epelbaum, 1976-1985* by Marjorie Agosin, translated by Janice Malloy, published by Williams-Wallace Publishers in Stratford, Ontario, Canada in 1989 (Williams-Wallace Publishers, Inc; POB 756, Stratford, Ontario N5A 4A0 Canada)

p. 79 Walter Benjamin's "angel of history" is described in his "Theses on the Philosophy of History," and quoted by Carolyn Forché in the epigraph to her volume named for his figure:

"This is how one pictures the angel of history. His face is turned toward the past. Where we perceive a chain of events, he sees one single catastrophe which keeps piling wreckage

*and hurls it in front of his feet. The angel would like to stay,
awaken the dead, and make whole what has been smashed.
But a storm is blowing in from Paradise; it has got caught in
his wings with such violence that the angel can no longer
close them. The storm irresistibly propels him into the future to
which his back is turned, while the pile of debris before him
grows skyward."*

Among the passengers aboard TWA Flight 800 that crashed
off Long Island in 1996 were the Forché scholar Constance
Coiner and her daughter Ana Duarte-Coiner.

Acknowledgements

The author wishes to offer sincere thanks to Molly Peacock, Ruth Stone, Maxine Kumin, and Laura Baudo Sillerman for their insight into and encouragement on this book. Thanks are also due to Deborah Fleming, Stephen Haven, and Sarah Wells at Ashland; the community of writers at the Wilkes University low-residency MA/ MFA program; and my colleagues at Binghamton University. As always, deepest gratitude to my family, especially Stephen, my children, and my sister Janine as well as my many friends who have provided support and sustaining encouragement, especially Catharine Foote, Peggy Sise, Nancy McKinley, and Neil Shepard.

Grateful acknowledgment is made to the editors of the following journals in which excerpts from the sequence first appeared:

Green Mountains Review: The section "Moon swims the night haze, pale" appeared under the title "Last July," the section "Do we ever/experience death" under the title "Dropping through Darkness."

New Letters: A Magazine of Writing & Art: The sections "What satiation could Eve have imagined" and "*My children named no one*" appeared under the titles "Appetite" and "The Disappeared."

Rosebud: The section "In this August meadow" appeared under the title "Baler."

ByLine Magazine: The section "oaks open their solicitous burgundy palms" appeared under the title "Autumn Pentacost." The section "The butterflies are drying" appeared under the title "Newly Opened."

Elsewhere: A Journal for the Literature of Place: "Euarctos americanus the American black bear," "May morning after rain," and "the pulmonary worms" sections first appeared here.

The Robert McGovern Publication Prize

The Robert McGovern Publication Prize is awarded to poets over 40 years of age who have published no more than one book. The prize was established in memory of Robert McGovern, poet, professor, co-founder of the Ashland Poetry Press, and long-time chair of the English Department at Ashland University. Manuscripts are submitted by nomination. The McGovern nominating panel currently consists of Annie Finch, Alice Fulton, Eamon Grennan, William Heyen, Andrew Hudgins, Richard Jackson, John Kinsella, Gerry LaFemina, Philip Levine, Robert Phillips, Vern Rutsala, Enid Shomer, and Gregory Wolfe. The Ashland Poetry Press editors also occasionally make an "Editor's Choice" selection for the McGovern series, outside of the regular nomination process.

Winners of the McGovern Prize are as follows:

Christine Gelineau, for *Appetite for the Divine*
(Editor's Choice, selected by Deborah Fleming)

Elizabeth Biller Chapman, for *Light Thickens*
(nominated by Enid Shomer)

Michael Miller, for *The Joyful Dark*
(Editor's Choice, selected by Stephen Haven)

Maria Terrone, for *A Secret Room in Fall*
(nominated by Gerry LaFemina)

Nathalie Anderson, for *Crawlers*
(nominated by Eamon Grennan)

A.V. Christie, for *The Housing*
(nominated by Eamon Grennan)

Jerry Harp, for *Gatherings*
(nominated by John Kinsella)